Team Smash

Five Amazing Girls, One Amazing Horse

By
Artemis Greenleaf

"The spirited horse, which will try to win the race of its own accord, will run even faster if encouraged."
Ovid

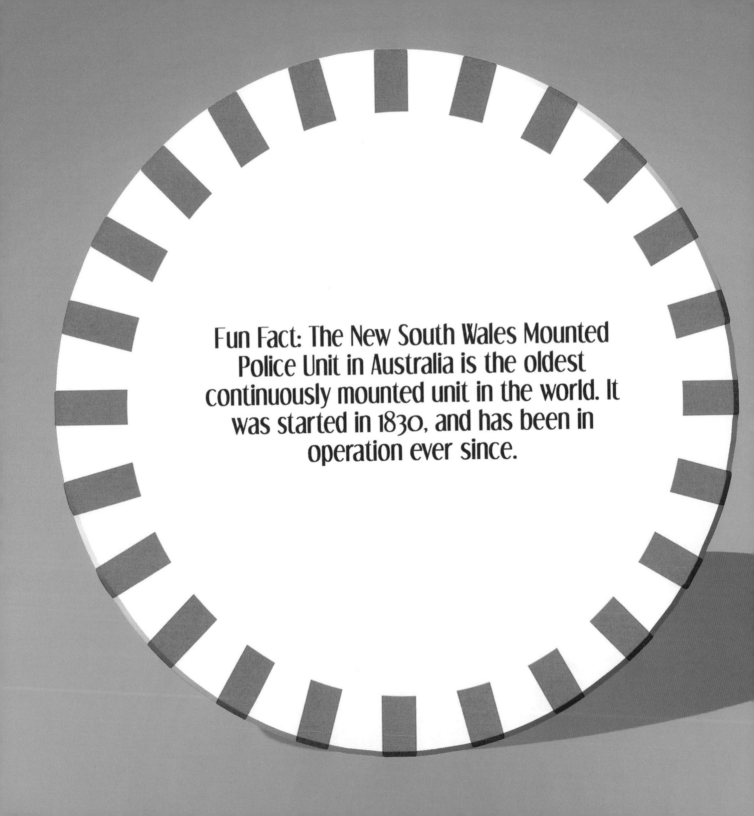

Fun Fact: The New South Wales Mounted Police Unit in Australia is the oldest continuously mounted unit in the world. It was started in 1830, and has been in operation ever since.

Part 1

Smash

Fun Fact: All
breed-registered
horses have the
same official birthday
– January 1.

It was a chilly February day in Pekin, Illinois, when a paint colt named "A Box Office Smash" was born at Stacey and Terry Kull's farm, Lost Creek Ranch.

Smash was born to be a show horse. He won first place as a yearling at the 2005 American Paint Horse Congress!
Even though he was very successful in the show ring, his trainer noticed there was something different about him. He didn't act quite like other horses.

As it turned out, Smash was deaf. It hadn't held him back in the show ring. Because he had done so well as a show horse, he became a dad. When his babies were also found to be deaf, Smash was retired. He went to live on a farm with Virginia Wagoner.

Virginia wanted nothing but the best for Smash. She knew that he could do so much more than hang around the farm and look handsome. When she heard about how the Houston Police Department's Mounted Patrol used natural horsemanship techniques, she thought she might have found a great opportunity for Smash.
Off he went to police horse school!

Smash became a cadet in July of 2013. He was the first HPD horse to have a ceremony when he graduated in September.

A Typical Day

For Smash

Breakfast at 6:00 AM. He gets crimped oats and rolled barley, along with a vitamin supplement. He loves to dunk his hay in his water bucket before he eats it!

Turn out with best buddy Figgy.
Horses are social animals that form long-term bonds. They remember both people and other horse friends they haven't seen for years.

Time to go to work! Smash and Officer Harris patrol whenever they are needed. One of their jobs is helping with crowd control during events like football games, street festivals, and parades.

Dinner is served at 6:00 PM. More oats and barley, vitamins, and pellets. There's a bedtime snack of delicious alfalfa hay at 8:30. Yum! Good night, Smash.

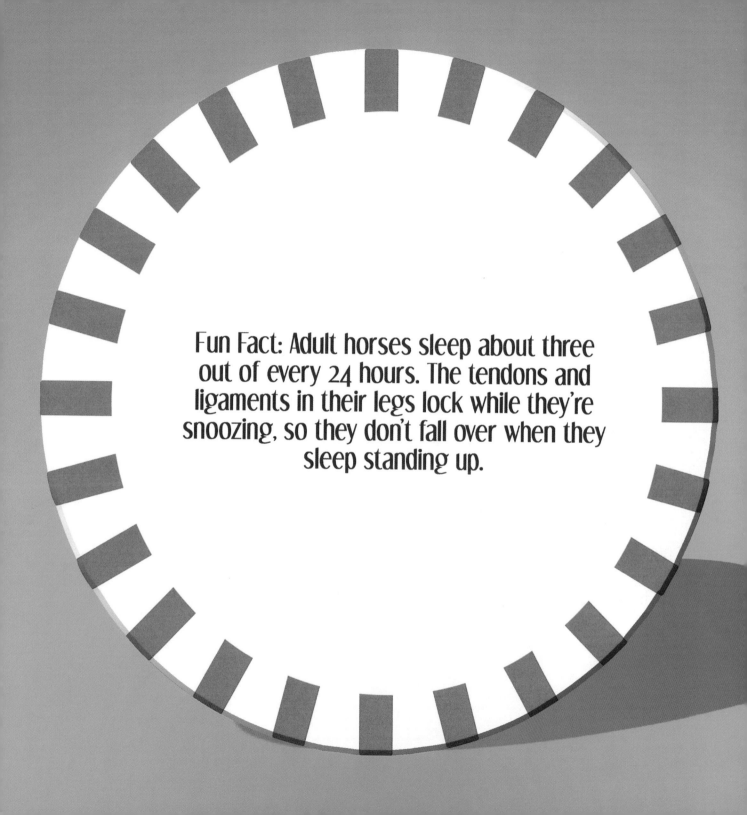

Fun Fact: Adult horses sleep about three out of every 24 hours. The tendons and ligaments in their legs lock while they're snoozing, so they don't fall over when they sleep standing up.

"The whole is greater than the sum of its parts."
Aristotle

Part 2

The Team

Katherine Richards had a birthday party at the Houston Police Mounted Division stables. Some of her friends from SIRE Therapeutic Horsemanship were there to celebrate with her. As the girls toured the barn, they saw Cadet Smash in his stall.

"Why doesn't he have a sponsor sign?" Katherine asked.

"He just hasn't found his sponsor yet," Sergeant Wills replied. "Sometimes it takes a little while."

"Smash is a special needs horse, and we're special needs girls – we should sponsor him!" the girls all agreed.

Katherine

Christi

Hillary

Meg

Ashley

SMASH GIRLS

It takes $5,000 per year to sponsor a patrol horse at HPD. The Smash Girls knew they had a lot of work to do. They held bake sales and special fund-raising events at three Smashburger locations. Team Smash was on TV, in newspapers and on social media. They started raising money in June, and by September, they'd raised $10,000. That's a lot of cupcakes!

Some of the money from the sale of this book will support Smash.

Molly White, a Texas artist, donated a painting of Smash to be used on posters for the Smash Girls to sell to raise money. Finding a way for Smash to sign the posters was tricky, but the staff figured it out. They put some paint on Smash's hoof, raised the poster off the ground just a little with a small stepstool, and had Smash put his foot on it. Perfect!

The Smash Girls were invited to New York City by the commander of the NYPD Mounted Unit, Deputy Inspector Barry Gelbman. Commander Gelbman had heard the girls speak at the North American Mounted Unit Commanders Association conference in March, and was so impressed that he wanted them to visit New York!

On their August, 2015 trip, they toured the NYPD stables, groomed and rode horses, then took a tour of New York harbor.

Fun Fact: Since 1938, the Royal Canadian Mounted Police only ride black horses.

"Amongst the qualities a hero should have, I would include determination, loyalty, courage, perseverance, patience, focus, intrepidity and selflessness." - Ricky Martin

Ashley Billard

Smash is the first animal I have ever met with special needs. Since he is deaf he has to try harder than the other horses. Even with his disability, he does an excellent job as a member of the Houston Mounted Patrol.

Smash is much bigger than you are. When you first met him, did that ever make you feel afraid?

I never felt afraid of Smash because my grandpa raised racehorses. Smash is very big but he looks friendly because of his gentle face.

What is your funniest story or happiest memory so far as a Smash Girl?

Smash loves attention and he will always nudge me with his head when I'm not giving him enough. He never let's me forget I'm a Smash Girl.

What piece of advice would you give someone who wants to make a difference, but doesn't know how?

Believe in yourself by being proud of who you are and show others how to believe in themselves. Start with one act of kindness and you will make a difference in this world.

Smash is a special horse, like I am a special girl. He has obstacles just like me, but he is still able to do his job.

What do you like to do when you aren't busy with Smash?

I work at Brookwood, play tennis and work on craft projects.

What is your funniest story or happiest memory so far as a Smash Girl?

That would be our trip to visit NYPD in New York City.

If you could have a superhero power, what would it be?

I would be able to fly.

Hillary Kern

Meg Norman

Smash is so handsome. Even though he is a special needs horse he wants to be a member of the Mounted Patrol. I think that is awesome!

What do you like to do when you aren't busy with Smash?

I love swimming, tennis, volleyball, and Zumba. I love to travel. I also do volunteer work at the Special Olympics office and at Artists in Action where we make cards for patients at the VA hospital and hospices.

What is one thing you'd like people to know about you?

I write poetry.

What piece of advice would you give someone who wants to make a difference, but doesn't know how?

Follow your heart, follow your dreams and don't let anyone tell you no!

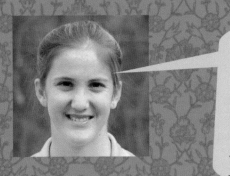

I love Smash! He has special needs just like me. I like to give him a bath and groom him. It is very relaxing for both of us. Smash is deaf but that doesn't matter because he can still be a great police horse. He can succeed at anything, like me. You just have to try.

What do you like to do when you aren't busy with Smash?

When I am not with Smash, I play a lot of tennis and compete all over the world. I also take horseback riding lessons and volunteer at the Houston Mounted Patrol. I like to rappel down buildings with Ashley. I love to travel and go to the theater. I have a job, too.

Smash is much bigger than you are. When you first met him, did that ever make you feel afraid?

At first all the horses made me a bit nervous because they are so big. The officers taught me how to be safe around horses and then I wasn't nervous anymore.

What piece of advice would you give someone who wants to make a difference, but doesn't know how?

My heart tells me what to do. Smash needed me and that is why my friends and I sponsored him. Pick a goal and keep trying until you get there. Sometimes it is hard, but keep trying.

Katherine Richards

Christi Roberts

Smash is a good horse and a good boy. He is fun and highly energetic. I want to support him because he has special needs just like me.

What is your funniest story or happiest memory so far as a Smash Girl?

It is fun to watch Smash get his teeth cleaned. He starts to fall asleep. Wish I could fall asleep when I get my teeth cleaned.

If you could have a superhero power, what would it be?

I would be invisible so I could go out on patrol with Smash.

What piece of advice would you give someone who wants to make a difference, but doesn't know how?

Be yourself and never give up.

I have been working with Smash since July of 2013.

You have said that being deaf might actually be an asset for Smash, because police horses spend a lot of time in noisy places. Noisy places often frighten horses. Does Smash have a calming effect on the other horses when there is more noise and activity than usual?

Since horses take cues from other horses, I definitely think that Smash has a calming effect, at least when it comes to his non-reaction to loud noises.

Riders can shift their weight, pull on the reins, or squeeze the horses with their legs to let them know where and how fast to go. Many riders use their voices as well. Since Smash can't hear you cluck to him to go faster, or say "Whoa!" to stop, what do you do instead?

Horses communicate with each other through mostly non-verbal means, so this is how we communicate with them. We use pressure and release. Pressure motivates and the release teaches. I squeeze my legs to ask Smash to go and once he starts moving, I stop squeezing. When I ask him to stop, I engage my seat, and lift the reins and apply pressure if needed till he stops. If I keep the same sequence, he will eventually stop when I engage my seat, and I don't even have to lift the reins.

If someone wants to visit Smash at the stables, what is his favorite treat? Where is the best place to pet him?

Smash loves peppermints and carrots and being scratched on his withers.

Officer Jeff Harris

Sergeant Leslie Wills

When Smash first came to HPD, he wasn't used to being turned out in a field with other horses. Sometimes he got beat up. How did you teach him how to be around them?

We started by putting him in a paddock next to the other horses and letting them learn to get along that way. Then we found some nonchalant horses to put with him and buddy up with. Once he had some friends and did not pose any threat to the leaders of the herd he was accepted.

As well as being deaf, Smash's job as a show horse was very different from his job as a police horse. How did you modify his training to help him understand his new career?

Smash was very good at his previous job as a fashion model. When he sees that camera come out, he immediately squares-up and has those ears forward. Transitioning into his new career as a Police Horse was a little stressful at first as he had to get out there and walk for several hours at a time. Exercise was not at the top of his priority list. But once he figured out that the more places he walked to, the more opportunities to meet people and thus more opportunities for treats or grass, he would walk all day.

What is one thing you want people to know about Smash?

Smash is so much more than just a horse, he really symbolizes that there are no challenges that are too great. And with a little help from your team you can Smash any barrier!!

You are a staunch advocate for people with intellectual disabilities, even starting your own foundation in 2006 to help them. What is one thing you would like people with special needs to know?

Everyone has "special needs." The important thing is not to let them define you. How you think and feel is very important and it matters. Find whatever makes you happy and just do it. It might be hard in the beginning, but stick with it. Your ability is endless.

Parents with special needs children have different challenges than parents without special needs children. What is one thing you would like special needs parents to know?

Children are a gift and each one is different. Look for the gift your special needs child has to offer and help them grow it. Don't be afraid to try new things. They may surprise you!

You are the main contact person for the Smash Girls, and you manage Smash's Facebook page. What is the best way for well-wishers, donors, or media to get in touch?

Please visit Smash's Facebook page.

Kim Richards

Molly Jackson White

I have been a fan of Smash and the Smash Girls since the beginning. I painted the limited edition portrait of Smash used on the posters the Smash Girls sell to raise money for his care. This special print is signed by both Smash and me!

Why did you choose the particular pose and background that you did to use for the Smash poster?

The photo I chose was my favorite photo on Smash's Facebook page. To me, it summed up what he does. The Houston skyline in the background and urban setting with him all tacked up and ready to go to protect his city told the story.

You have your own horses. Do you often use them as models?

Believe it or not, I don't paint a lot of horses, even though I have five of them in my backyard! Horses are one of the most difficult subjects to paint for me. Their bodies are constructed in such a way that if you are just slightly "off" with your drawing, it is noticeable to a horse person. It just doesn't look right. I spent hours and hours getting Smash just right with a charcoal drawing first. The painting was the easy part.

What is one thing you'd like aspiring artists to know?

I have always loved art, but never felt good enough to really pursue it as a profession. What I discovered is that if it's something you love, you should go for it! You will get better quickly by practicing. Like anything, whether it is tennis, playing the piano, or other skills, you must practice.

I donated Smash to the Houston Police Department.

How did you hear about HPD's mounted patrol natural horsemanship program?

From my friend, Cris Van Horn.

What made you think this might be a good home for Smash?

I knew he would be great at it because of his laid back personality and love of children. And being deaf, the noise of crowds and traffic wouldn't bother him. While he was here, he gave my foster daughters a lot of confidence and loved to be brushed and bathed by them. A gentle giant even though he was still a stallion. That's why I knew he was a special horse.

What is one thing you would like people to know about paint horses?

Paint horses are so very versatile and willing to please. They generally will be able to do just about anything you ask.

Virginia Wagoner

Smash is an amazing horse. But he can't do it alone. People are responsible for feeding him and his buddies, mucking out stalls, bathing and grooming, trimming hooves, and cleaning saddles. The horses attend a monthly training workshop. Whenever Smash and friends are going out on patrol, they get a ride there in the horse trailer, so someone has to drive the truck. None of this smashing story would be possible without this crew!

Coloring

Pages

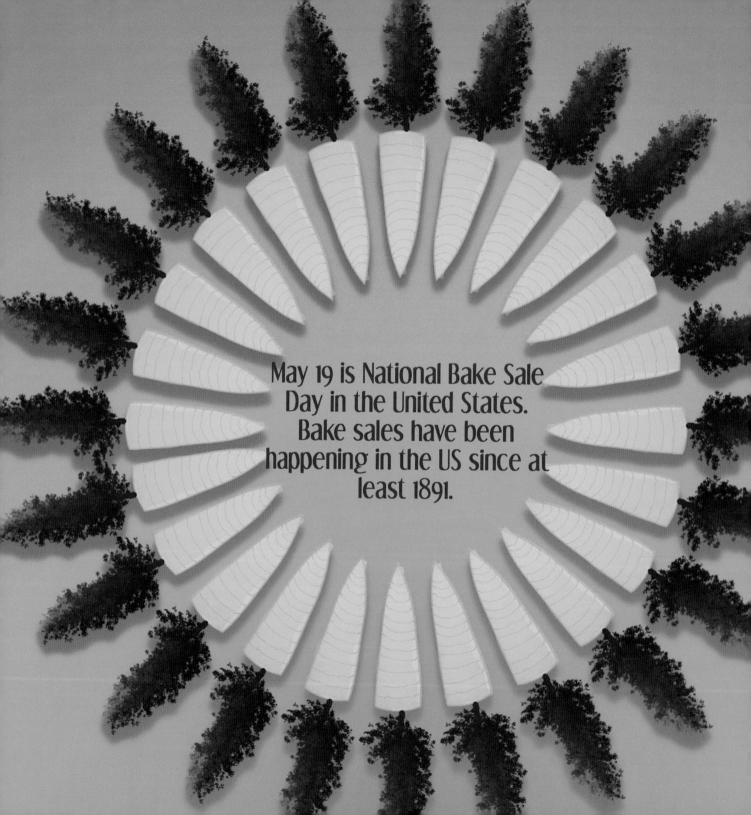

May 19 is National Bake Sale
Day in the United States.
Bake sales have been
happening in the US since at
least 1891.

Fun Fact: Therapeutic riding, or hippotherapy, has been used since ancient times to help people with physical or mental disabilities, emotional trauma, or neurological disorders.

Although the NYPD was using officers on horseback to patrol Central Park when it opened in 1858, the mounted unit wasn't formally organized until 1871. Some people call NYPD mounted officers "10-Foot Cops."

Fun Fact: As of 2015, there are about a million horses in the state of Texas. Almost half of those are Quarter Horses.

The nomadic Comanche tribes of the southern North American plains liked paint and pinto horses more than any other color. A horse that was mostly white, but had a colored area on top of his head and ears (called a Medicine Hat), was the most prized of all.

Fun Fact: Natural Horsemanship is way of training horses where people work to create a partnership with them. The horses do what they're asked because they like and trust the person asking, not because they are forced. People who use this kind of training are often called "Horse Whisperers."

An average-sized horse will typically eat about 25 lb (11 kg) of hay and grain per day. A draft horse can eat more than twice that. The Budweiser Clydesdales each eat about five gallons of grain, plus 50-60 pounds of hay per day.

Fun Fact: The Akhal-Teke is a
breed of horse that has a
metallic sheen. This is due
to its translucent hair.

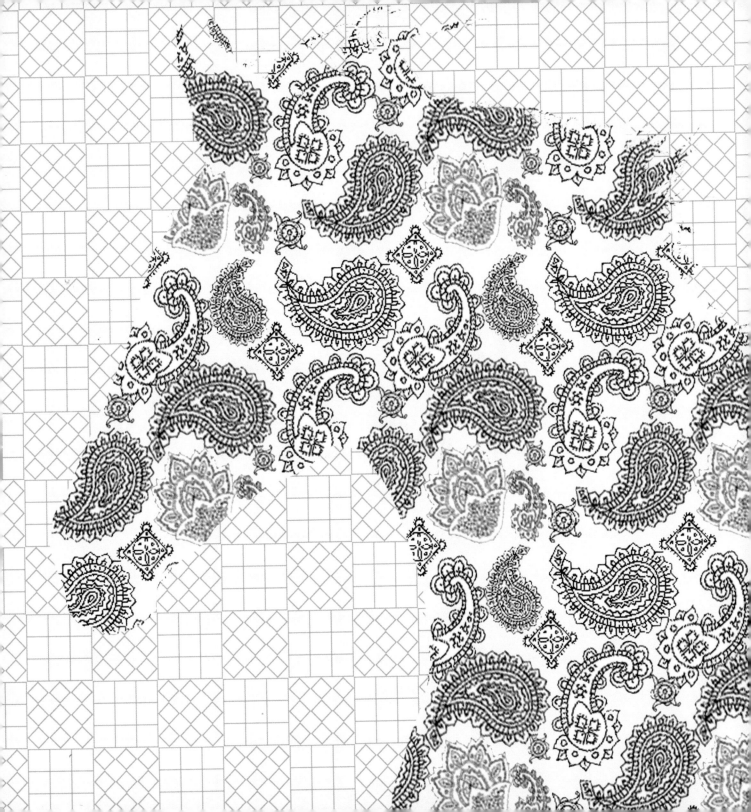

Fun Fact: The earliest known ancestor of the horse, Hyracotherium (also know as Eohippus), lived during the Eocne Epoch, about 50 million years ago. It was about the size of a cocker spaniel.

"Whether you think you can,
or you think you can't - you're right."
Henry Ford

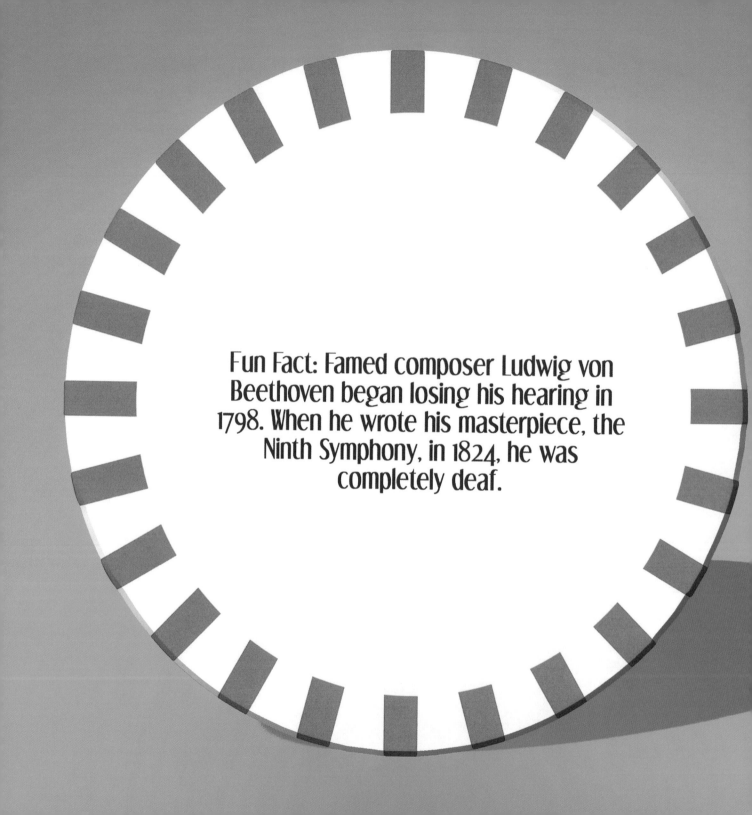

Fun Fact: Famed composer Ludwig von Beethoven began losing his hearing in 1798. When he wrote his masterpiece, the Ninth Symphony, in 1824, he was completely deaf.

Acknowledgments

This book would not have been possible without the copious and invaluable assistance of Houston Police Mounted Patrol Sergeant Leslie Wills and Smash Girls mom, Kim Richards. Your dedication is inspiring!

Also, I'd like to send a shout-out to the Smash Girls' parents. When you found out your daughters had intellectual disabilities, you could have kept them at home. But you didn't – you got them involved and doing things out in the world. Otherwise, they wouldn't have met each other. When they wanted to sponsor Smash, you could have quietly written checks. But you didn't – you decided to let the girls do it themselves. And that space is where the magic happened.

Thanks to my friend and fellow author, Monica Shaughnessy, who brainstormed with me at lunch during the Houston Writer's Guild conference to come up with the idea of writing a book about Smash.

As always, love to my family for putting up with this crazy writing business.

Other Books by Artemis Greenleaf

For Younger Readers
Brain's Vacation
Carl the Vegetarian Vampire

For Teens and Tweens
Earthbound
Cheval Bayard
Confessions of a Troll
Exit Point

For Adults
The Hanged Man's Wife
The Magician's Children
Color Me Blackthorne

As Coda Sterling
Dragon by Knight
Dragon Killer

Anthologies
Space City 6
Tides of Impossibility
First Last Forever

Artemis Greenleaf has always been fascinated by the mysterious, and she devoured fairy tales, folk tales and ghost stories since before she could read. In 1995, she had a near-death experience which turned her perception of the world upside down. She lived to tell the tale (and often does, in one form or another), and went on to marry an alien. She lives in the suburban wilds of Houston, Texas with her husband, two children and assorted pets. She writes novels, short stories, and non-fiction, and her work has appeared in magazines and anthologies. For more

If you enjoyed this book, please consider leaving a review at your favorite book sharing site. Thank you!

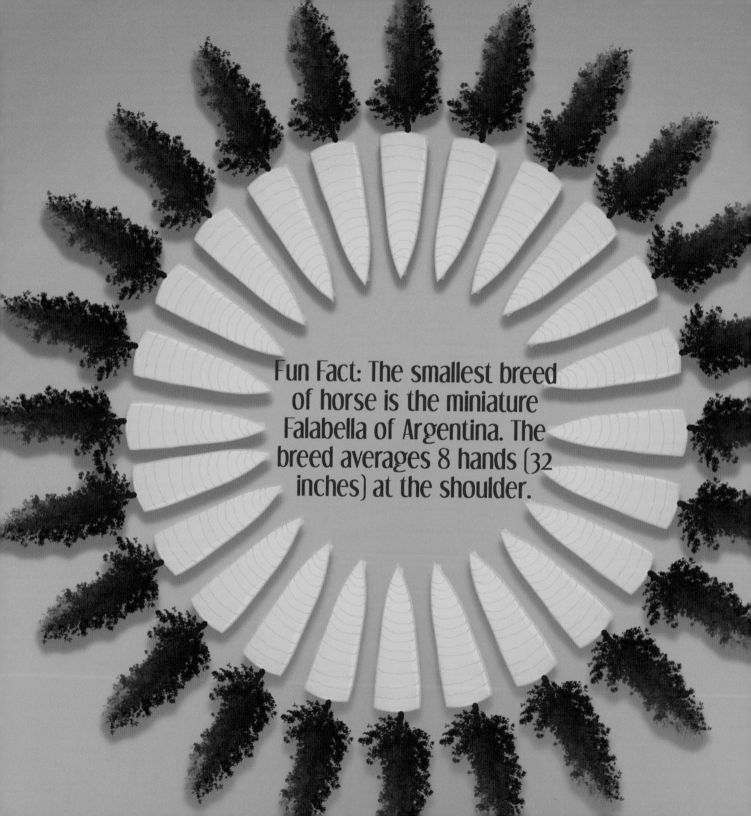

Fun Fact: The smallest breed of horse is the miniature Falabella of Argentina. The breed averages 8 hands (32 inches) at the shoulder.

Team Smash:
Five Amazing Girls, One Amazing Horse
By
Artemis Greenleaf
SOFTCOVER EDITION
PUBLISHED BY:
Black Mare Books
Houston, Texas
www.blackmarebooks.com

ISBN: 978-1-941502-83-9

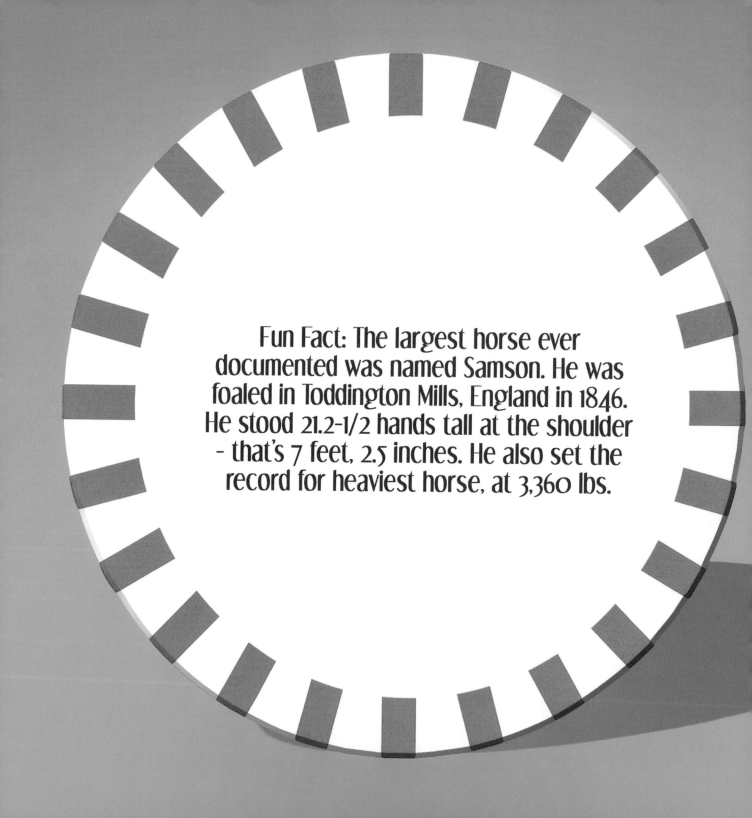

Fun Fact: The largest horse ever documented was named Samson. He was foaled in Toddington Mills, England in 1846. He stood 21.2-1/2 hands tall at the shoulder - that's 7 feet, 2.5 inches. He also set the record for heaviest horse, at 3,360 lbs.

Photo Credits

Smash Girls' Portraits and Pictures with Smash
Provided by Photos by Rovo (http://www.photosbyrovo.com/)

Photo of Lost Creek Ranch and Smash as a Yearling
Provided by Stacey Kull

Photo of Virginia Wagoner
Provided by Virginia Wagoner

All Other Photos
Provided by the Houston Police Department

Animals at the Houston Zoo
paint their own art pieces
that are sold to help with
their care and feeding.

RESOURCES

Want to learn more?

Smash's Facebook page:
https://www.facebook.com/SmashTheHoustonMountedPatrolHorse/

Smash's graduation ceremony:
https://youtu.be/PFi32X6tceo

Richards Family Foundation:
http://www.richardsfamilyfoundation.org/

HPD's Mounted Patrol website:
http://www.houstontx.gov/police/mounted/horses.htm

Houston Police Foundation:
http://www.houstonpolicefoundation.org/

SIRE Therapeutic Horsemanship:
http://sire-htec.org/

Pat Parelli Natural Horsemanship:
http://www.parelli.com/

Molly White Fine Art:
http://mollywhitefineart.com/

Made in the USA
Charleston, SC
21 October 2016